In Loving Memory

Copyright © 2019 Lollys Publishing

All rights reserved.

ISBN: 9781912641529

A Celebration of the Life of

....

Born On

....

Passed Away On

....

Those we love don't go away,

They walk beside us

every day.

Unseen, Unheard,

But always near.

Still loved, still missed,

and very dear.

Name, Address
Thoughts & Memories

Name, Address
Thoughts & Memories

Name, Address
Thoughts & Memories

Name, Address
Thoughts & Memories

....

....

....

....

....

....

....

....

Name, Address
Thoughts & Memories

Name, Address
Thoughts & Memories

Name, Address
Thoughts & Memories

Name, Address
Thoughts & Memories

Name, Address
Thoughts & Memories

Name, Address
Thoughts & Memories

Name, Address
Thoughts & Memories

Name, Address
Thoughts & Memories

Name, Address
Thoughts & Memories

Name, Address
Thoughts & Memories

....

....

....

....

....

....

....

....

Name, Address
Thoughts & Memories

....

....

....

....

....

....

....

....

....

Name, Address
Thoughts & Memories

Name, Address
Thoughts & Memories

Name, Address
Thoughts & Memories

Name, Address
Thoughts & Memories

Name, Address
Thoughts & Memories

Name, Address
Thoughts & Memories

....

....

....

....

....

....

....

....

....

Name, Address
Thoughts & Memories

Name, Address
Thoughts & Memories

Name, Address
Thoughts & Memories

Name, Address
Thoughts & Memories

Name, Address
Thoughts & Memories

Name, Address
Thoughts & Memories

Name, Address
Thoughts & Memories

Name, Address
Thoughts & Memories

Name, Address
Thoughts & Memories

Name, Address
Thoughts & Memories

Name, Address
Thoughts & Memories

....

....

....

....

....

....

....

....

Name, Address
Thoughts & Memories

Name, Address
Thoughts & Memories

Name, Address
Thoughts & Memories

Name, Address
Thoughts & Memories

Name, Address
Thoughts & Memories

Name, Address
Thoughts & Memories

Name, Address
Thoughts & Memories

Name, Address
Thoughts & Memories

Name, Address
Thoughts & Memories

Name, Address
Thoughts & Memories

Name, Address
Thoughts & Memories

Name, Address
Thoughts & Memories

Name, Address
Thoughts & Memories

Name, Address
Thoughts & Memories

Name, Address
Thoughts & Memories

Name, Address
Thoughts & Memories

Name, Address
Thoughts & Memories

Name, Address
Thoughts & Memories

Name, Address
Thoughts & Memories

Name, Address
Thoughts & Memories

Name, Address
Thoughts & Memories

Name, Address
Thoughts & Memories

Name, Address
Thoughts & Memories

Name, Address
Thoughts & Memories

Name, Address
Thoughts & Memories

Name, Address
Thoughts & Memories

Name, Address
Thoughts & Memories

Name, Address
Thoughts & Memories

Name, Address
Thoughts & Memories

Name, Address
Thoughts & Memories

Name, Address
Thoughts & Memories

Name, Address
Thoughts & Memories

Name, Address
Thoughts & Memories

Name, Address
Thoughts & Memories

Name, Address
Thoughts & Memories

Name, Address
Thoughts & Memories

Name, Address
Thoughts & Memories

Name, Address
Thoughts & Memories

Name, Address
Thoughts & Memories

....

....

....

....

....

....

....

....

....

Name, Address
Thoughts & Memories

Name, Address
Thoughts & Memories

Name, Address
Thoughts & Memories

Name, Address
Thoughts & Memories

Name, Address
Thoughts & Memories

Name, Address
Thoughts & Memories

Name, Address
Thoughts & Memories

Name, Address
Thoughts & Memories

Name, Address
Thoughts & Memories

Name, Address
Thoughts & Memories

....

....

....

....

....

....

....

....

....

Name, Address
Thoughts & Memories

Name, Address
Thoughts & Memories

Name, Address
Thoughts & Memories

Name, Address
Thoughts & Memories

Name, Address
Thoughts & Memories

....

....

....

....

....

....

....

....

....

Name, Address
Thoughts & Memories

Name, Address
Thoughts & Memories

Name, Address
Thoughts & Memories

Name, Address
Thoughts & Memories

Name, Address
Thoughts & Memories

Name, Address
Thoughts & Memories

Name, Address
Thoughts & Memories

Name, Address
Thoughts & Memories

Milton Keynes UK
Ingram Content Group UK Ltd.
UKHW030618080224
437390UK00001B/1